CAPTAIN WILLIAM MOORE

The incredible Captain Moore delivered
mail by dog team through 600 miles of Yukon
wilderness when he was 74.

Norman Hacking

Design by John Moutray

FRONT COVER
The commercial sternwheel era on the Fraser River which began in 1858 ended in 1925 when the *Skeena* became the last of the colorful vessels to ply the waterway. But the throb of the paddlewheel hadn't been totally stilled.

The Canadian Government operated a work boat, the *Samson V* shown on the front cover, to help keep the river free of debris. In 1980 she, too, was retired, the last steam-powered paddlewheeler in the Pacific Northwest.

Fortunately, she has been preserved at New Westminster. As the *Samson V* Maritime Museum, she is a popular tourist attraction.

BACK COVER
Dog team on a Yukon trail, a scene very familiar to Captain Moore who was mushing mail 600 miles when he was 74. (See page 54.)

PHOTO CREDITS
Canadian Government Travel Bureau: 58-59; Provincial Archives of B.C.: 6-7, 12-13, 16-17, 19, 24, 26-27, 30-31, 34, 36-37, 42-43, 50; Tourism B.C.: 24 (lower); University of Alaska: title page; University of Washington: 46; Vancouver Public Library: 12 (top right, bottom), 52; Yukon Archives: 53.

COPYRIGHT © 1993 Norman Hacking

Canadian Cataloguing in Publication Data

Hacking, Norman R., 1912 -
    Captain William Moore

ISBN 1-895811-02-3

1.Moore, William, 1822-1909. 2. Frontier
and pioneer life — British Columbia. 3.
British Columbia — Gold discoveries. 4.
British Columbia — Biography. I. Title.
F1088.M65H33 1993   C92-091763-1

HERITAGE HOUSE PUBLISHING COMPANY LTD.
Box 1228, Station A, Surrey. B.C. V3S 2B3

Printed in Canada.

CONTENTS

Captain Moore's Country 4

Chapter One 6

Chapter Two 19

Chapter Three 30

Chapter Four 42

Chapter Five 52

On White Pass Summit, April 1, 1898, Klondike-bound stampeders
experience the harsh Yukon climate so familiar to Captain Moore. Another
view of this route, discovered by Moore, is on page 46.

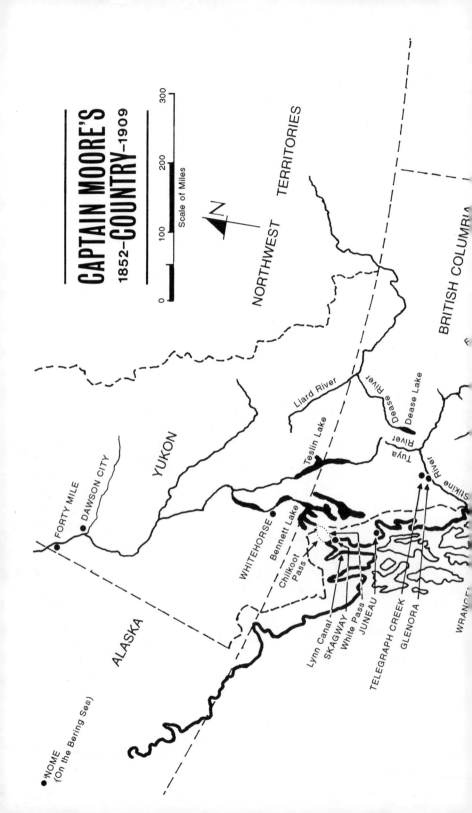

CAPTAIN MOORE'S
COUNTRY–1909
1852–

Scale of Miles

0   100   200   300

N

NORTHWEST TERRITORIES

BRITISH COLUMBIA

ALASKA

YUKON

NOME
(On the Bering Sea)

FORTY MILE

DAWSON CITY

WHITEHORSE

Bennett Lake

Chilkoot Pass

Lynn Canal

SKAGWAY

White Pass

JUNEAU

TELEGRAPH CREEK

GLENORA

WRANGEL

Liard River

Teslin Lake

Dease River

Dease Lake

Tuya River

Stikine River

Drawn by John Moutray   Information by A. Byrne

A sketch of B.C.'s capital, Victoria, in July 1858. Three
months previously it had been a quiet Hudson's Bay
Company trading post, but with discovery of gold on the
Fraser River some 30,000 treasure hunters stampeded to
the area, among them Captain William Moore. He arrived
from San Francisco with his wife, three young children
and an assortment of goats and hogs.

New Westminster, below in 1863, was Victoria's rival and
the capital of the Crown Colony of British Columbia. From
the community sternwheelers plied up the Fraser River to
Yale, and downstream to the Strait of Georgia,
then to Victoria.

CHAPTER ONE

One of British Columbia's most colorful and adventurous pioneers was Captain William Moore. He came to B.C. during the 1852 gold rush to the Queen Charlotte Islands and thereafter for over half a century took part in every stampede, including the Fraser River in 1858, the Stikine River, the Big Bend of the Columbia River, the Cariboo, the Omineca, the Cassiar, the Klondike and, finally, Nome in 1900 when he was 78. He discovered the White Pass which became the main portal to the Yukon and years before the famous Klondike rush staked 160 acres on which grew the community of Skagway.

An unknown sternwheeler at the landing in Yale when the community was the gateway to the Cariboo and Barkerville, 400 miles to the northward. The church near left center is St. John the Divine, built in 1860. Still in use, it is the oldest church in B.C. on its original site.

Wherever gold was found Moore would arrive with supplies, moving them by sailing barge, packmule, canoe or sternwheel steamer. He pioneered navigation on the Stikine River where hazards included hostile Indians who told him to leave since his paddlewheel steamer was scaring the fish. Moore was not one to be intimidated and remained, although other Indians later killed one of his three sons. As a sailor and river steamboatman he had few equals, while his feats of endurance as an old man on wilderness trails were incredible.

A loving family man, he had three daughters and four sons. The latter were a credit to their father, accompanying him on many of his expeditions and opening up many unexplored areas themselves. He made at least three fortunes but died comparatively poor in Victoria in 1909, having lived 87 adventurous years.

Captain William Moore, or Bill Moore, as he was known throughout the West, was a native of Hanover, Germany, where he was born on March 30, 1822. He never lost his strong German accent. Friends and rivals called him the "Flying Dutchman," a name he revelled in, for he gave it to two of his vessels. He and his sons were voluminous letter writers and also kept personal diaries so that many of the family records have been preserved.

He had little formal education, but his education in the university of experience was more than sufficient to make him an outstanding figure in the untamed West of the late Nineteenth Century. The sea was in his blood for as early as age seven he sailed on schooners in the North Sea. His sea roving eventually brought him to New Orleans about 1846, where he married his loving and long-suffering wife, Hendrika. He served in two boats on the Lower Mississippi and took part in the Mexican War of 1848 aboard USS *Lawrence* in the Gulf of Mexico.

His eldest son, John, known usually as "J.W.," or "Johnnie," was born at New Orleans in 1848, and that year Moore became a naturalized American citizen. Since he subsequently spent most of his life in B.C., he also proudly claimed to be a British subject when it suited his purpose. At one time when he secured a contract to carry the Royal Mail in British Columbia, a rival bidder protested that Captain Moore was a foreigner. He replied that he was a British subject, having been born in Hanover when it belonged to the British crown.

In 1851 his restless spirit took him to San Francisco, attracted by the tales of wealth which had been won from the Sierra Nevada. Too late to reap the treasure of the California gold rush, he resolved never again to be late when lured by the cry of gold. He never was.

After a brief and unsuccessful gold hunting expedition to Klamath River in Oregon, he was excited by reports of a gold discovery in the remote Queen Charlotte Islands. Early in 1852 a sailor who had been in the service of the Hudson's Bay Company arrived in San Francisco and reported that gold had been found at Englefield Harbor, on the west shore of Moresby Island, in the Queen Charlottes. On the evidence of some specimens he showed, 65 people, including Bill Moore, embarked on March 29 on board the brig *Tepic*. They arrived safely at their destination, but the gold proved scarce, the Haida Indians menacing, and after a month of prospecting they returned to San Francisco.

Undismayed by this failure, Captain Moore gathered his wife and child and sailed away to Peru where he had heard tales that the wealth of the Incas awaited the adventurous. He procured a schooner and engaged in the coasting trade. At Callao, Peru, in 1854 his second son, William D. Moore, was born. Mrs. Moore was so frightened by one of the frequent revolutions occurring in the country that she persuaded her husband to return to San Francisco in the spring of 1856. He settled on barren Goat Island, now crossed by the Bay Bridge, where he raised goats.

Early in 1858 he heard reports of rich gold discoveries in the remote Fraser River region. He quickly disposed of his property, then loaded goats and hogs into the schooner, along with his growing family, (baby Henrietta was born at Goat Island), and set sail for Victoria on what was then the Colony of Vancouver Island. It was to be the nearest place that he could call "home" for the rest of his wandering life.

In the frantic little goldrush town he built a small house for his brood and a 15-ton barge which he named the *Blue Bird*. During that hectic year, when some 30,000 gold-seekers poured into the sleepy port of Victoria from California, Moore found wealth not in the bars of the Fraser but in providing transport up the river to Fort Hope.

Sailing and rowing a clumsy barge against the current was brutal work, even for such an expert sailor as Bill Moore. As a consequence, in 1859 he used his profits to order a proper sternwheel steamboat. It was launched in October from Trahey's shipyard in Victoria and christened the *Henrietta*. She was only 73 feet long, and prior to the arrival of her engines was operated under sail as far up as Port Douglas at the head of Harrison Lake.

Moore assigned the job of piloting her to Captain "Gassy Jack" Deighton, later renowned as the first property-owner of the village of Granville, now the city of Vancouver. When finally equipped with power the *Henrietta* drew only 20 inches of water with 40 tons of freight. She was the first of many sternwheelers owned or operated by Bill Moore.

The *Henrietta* proved a money-maker, but she wasn't powerful enough or big enough to satisfy Captain Moore's ambitions, especially with freight rates $25 a ton from New Westminster to Hope. He managed to take her up to Yale in February 1860, which was the occasion for a real wing-ding of a party. According to the Yale correspondent of the Victoria *Colonist:*

"Her arrival was the signal for a general suspension of business. All was excitement such as I have never before witnessed in Yale. Anvils were made to answer the purpose of cannon, and quite a brisk firing was kept up during the afternoon. A large banner was displayed on the river front upon which the words 'Welcome *Henrietta'* but echoed the heart-felt sentiment of the entire community. Capt. Moore deserves much credit for his untiring energy and perseverence, for he has established and maintained the position that Yale is accessible by steam, at this, the worst season. In the evening a collation to Capt. Moore and his officers rendered the occasion one that will not soon be forgotten."

In July 1860 Moore sold the *Henrietta* to the opposition and promptly used the proceeds to build a bigger and better boat, the 92-foot *Flying Dutchman*. She was launched at Victoria in September with the usual champagne and festivities. She ran her trial trip in January 1861, and Moore soon made a deal with his competitors on the river to keep up the passenger fares and freight rates and split the profits. He operated chiefly on the Harrison Lake route, between Harrisonmouth and Port Douglas. When light, the *Flying Dutchman* drew only 5 inches of water.

The year 1862 started off with cutthroat competition on the Fraser River, so when Moore heard that placer gold had been found on the bars of the Stikine River in far-off Northwestern B.C. he couldn't resist the promise of instant wealth. He built a flat-bottomed barge at Victoria which he named the *J. W. Moore,* and in June set out with 60 passengers in the *Flying Dutchman,* towing the barge well laden with freight.

This voyage was perilous in the extreme for so fragile a craft as a light-draft sternwheeler. It entailed battling 300 miles of poorly surveyed, treacherous channels northward along Vancouver Island, then crossing such open waters as Queen Charlotte Sound, Milbanke Sound and Dixon Entrance. But Moore was never one to run away from risk, and he arrived safely at sleepy Fort Wrangell, port of entry for the Stikine River which flows through both British Columbia and Alaska.

The Stikine was considered by most river boatmen to be the most dangerous navigable stream in British Columbia because of its turbulent currents and narrow gorges. A United States government report described its perils:

"The velocity and strength of the current throughout the whole length of the river is its most remarkable feature. Without any falls or impediments the current sweeps down with great uniformity, and when the bed or banks are not suitable for towing or tracking the only way to force a boat up is by poles. The velocity of the current was measured at several places and averages four or five miles an hour."

Captain Bill Moore tackled this dangerous river without any foreknowledge of its perils, relying solely upon his own judgment as a river boatman. He managed to reach Buck's Bar in three days, a distance of about 140 miles. It was here that the first gold discovery had been made by fur trader Alexandre "Buck" Choquette.

Moore charged as much as the traffic would bear, which was only natural considering the risks he was running — and the fact that he had a monopoly on the river. He charged $100 a ton for freight, $20 per man without food or berth, and five cents a pound for personal effects. He made what was considered a fortune in those days — about $20,000 profit for the short summer season.

On numerous occasions he had trouble with the natives who demanded that he stop running the "Fire Boat" on the river. They claimed it made so much noise it would drive the fish and game out of the country. A big meeting was held, accompanied by much eloquent speechifying by the Tlingits and threats of reprisals. To soothe the hostile group Moore purchased $200 worth of Hudson's Bay blankets which he distributed among the tribesmen.

The Stikine diggings proved shallow, however, and at the end of the season the *Flying Dutchman* sailed back to Victoria with most of the miners aboard and most of their hard-earned gold dust in Captain Moore's strong box. His gamble had paid off. Then when he reached home he found there another bonus — a further addition to his family, daughter Wilhelmina. She was the second member of the family to be born at Victoria. The first had been his third son, Henry.

There was no rush of miners to the Stikine in 1863, so Captain Moore returned to the Fraser River trade with the *Flying Dutchman* and *J. W. Moore*, in which he had installed a twin-screw engine for service on Harrison Lake. But his ambitions were far from satisfied. With the profits he had made on the Stikine he ordered from James Trahey the largest sternwheeler yet built for the Fraser

She was launched at Victoria in July 1863 as the *Alexandra*, named in honour of the Princess of Wales. However, non-arrival of her machinery and litigation between Moore and Trahey delayed her completion for a year. There were other financial problems as well. Competition between the various Fraser River steamboats was so keen in 1863 that none made a profit. At one time fares between New Westminster and Yale were down to 25 cents. Several boats were laid up, some of the owners went bankrupt, and Moore sold the *J. W. Moore* for use as a towboat on Puget Sound.

Conditions on early sternwheelers were not always the most

Captain William Irving, above, was the most popular and successful of all gold-rush skippers, and always emerged victorious from the ruthless rate wars with Moore. He was the first president of New Westminster city council and when he died the *Mainland Guardian* edged its advertisements and news columns with black in tribute. His house has survived and is open to the public. (See page 34.)

Captain Irving's sternwheeler *Onward* at Yale in 1868. In 1865 Mrs. Moore sailed on her from New Westminster on the first part of her journey to Barkerville during one of Captain Moore's bankruptcies.

Top Left: Of all those who took part in the Fraser River gold rush and were associated with Captains Moore and Irving, a man named Jack Deighton has the most impressive memorial. Unsuccessful in his quest for gold he became a riverboat captain for both Moore and Irving.

In 1867 he left the river and on the shore of Burrard Inlet built a shake-roofed saloon, the Globe. Around the saloon appeared other buildings, opposite, and since Jack Deighton was a talkative man, the settlement was named "Gastown" in his honor. In 1870, however, residents changed the name to the more dignified Granville, then in 1886 to Vancouver, now Canada's third largest city.

comfortable, as is revealed by an announcement that appeared in the New Westminster *British Columbian* late in 1863:

"The undersigned Passengers on the splendid steamboat *Flying Dutchman* on her last trip down from Harrison River, would tender our hearty thanks to Capt. Bill Moore for the high-toned and elegant manner with which we were treated on the trip. We left Harrison River about 12 o'clock on Tuesday. About 1 o'clock on the same day the boat made such rapid progress that we were laid up on a bar to prevent her making 'lightning speed' to New Westminster.

"On that Bar we rested heavily for the space of twenty-one hours, sleeping lightly in chairs, on board, and in bunks designed for weary miners. Soon after we left the bar our polite and accommodating Captain ran his barge into a snag, which ran into the barge hard enough to dump her cargo of horned individuals into the chuck.

"After this our Captain, in a spirit of thanksgiving, ordered that no more grub should be served on his boat; and we proceeded to New Westminster, where we arrived about 7 p.m., with appetites sufficiently keen to do ample justice to the best dinner ever set at the Colonial. For all of which we desire to tender to Capt. Moore the renewed assurances of our highest regard and most distinguished consideration. And to the public we would say travel with Bill Moore when you see either one of us go aboard his boat, and not till then."

The big event in 1864 was the completion of the *Alexandra*, but she was in no way as lavishly fitted as Moore had intended. The vessel was modelled on a Mississippi River boat, with two tall stacks, or "chimneys," as they were called. As originally planned she was to have stateroom accommodation for 58 passengers.

The after part of her hull was to be fitted as a ladies' cabin, and the center occupied by the main saloon, which was lined on each side by 15 staterooms. A large pantry and kitchen adjoined the saloon, while forward were the boilers and fire-rooms. A second cabin, in the forecastle, had a capacity for 40 passengers.

On the main deck, the after part was occupied by the engine room, forward of which was the well-stocked bar, with companion ways to the saloon deck and upper deck. The latter included a promenade, the captain's and purser's cabins, and the pilothouse forward. The pilothouse boasted a steam gauge, an innovation on Fraser River boats. The *Alexandra* had four boilers and three separate sternwheels, each of which could be run independently. Her 145-hp engines were described as being "of the most powerful and elegant description," and she had a freight capacity of 400 tons.

Alas, the *Alexandra* was doomed to failure. She was expensive to operate and her hull was weak. Worse, she arrived just as the mine traffic began to decline. It was the intention of Moore and his partner, Captain Asbury Insley, to run her direct from Victoria to Yale, connecting with the *Flying Dutchman* at Harrisonmouth at the junction of the Harrison and Fraser Rivers. But she proved too big and unwieldy for the up-river trade except at high water, and made only two or three through trips.

On one trip down-river Captain Moore made the run from Yale to New Westminster in only six hours. From Yale to Harrisonmouth he averaged 21½ miles an hour. Speed, unfortunately, was not sufficient to make the *Alexandra* pay. On July 12, 1864, he announced that she would start a service from Victoria to Olympia. In August there was a short-lived gold excitement at Leech River, near Sooke, and Moore, never one to resist a gold rush, ran his ship from Victoria to Sooke for a time.

But his creditors were closing in. He had already lost the *Flying Dutchman* and debts were piling up against the *Alexandra.* Moore made a final attempt to compete in the Fraser River trade, but the odds were against him. On September 25, 1864, he crossed the Strait of Georgia from New Westminster with 40 passengers aboard the *Alexandra* and a barge in tow. He had been warned that sheriff's officers were waiting for him at Victoria so he decided to make a run for the American side.

He cast off his tow at Esquimalt, put his passengers ashore, and found a haven at Port Angeles. His creditors chartered the *Flying Dutchman* at New Westminster and in the best Wild-West tradition sallied forth in pursuit, but failed to make an arrangement. The debt was said to be $17,000.

Moore's flight to the American side, though, did him no good for the crew sued for back wages. The United States marshal seized the *Alexandra* and she was laid up at Penn's Cove, Whidbey Island. Captain Moore camped nearby, where he was soon joined by his wife, his brood of children, and the family goats.   ˎ

For several months the vessel lay at Whidbey Island, until one night a party from Victoria, headed by Captain Moore's erstwhile partner, Captain Insley, came alongside. They boarded the *Alexandra,* telling the U.S. marshal, who was aboard guarding the vessel, that they had been engaged to put the machinery in first class shape.

While the work was going on a fire was placed under the boiler, and when sufficient steam developed the marshal was told that a trial run was necessary. He gave permission but as soon as the boat was underway her course was set for Victoria, the vigorous protests of the marshal being ignored. On the vessel's arrival at Victoria the fuming marshal was ordered ashore since he had no authority in British waters. The hijacking did no good to Captain Moore, for his $50,000 ship was sold at auction for only $8,000. On

February 22, 1865, he was adjudged bankrupt in the Victoria court.

The indomitable Moore, however, quickly got back into business. He acquired a small sloop and took his family, household effects and goats to New Westminster. Here he was able to find a house in time for the arrival of another little Moore, Bernard. Shortly after his move to New Westminster, Captain Moore acquired a large barge called the *Lady of the Lake* which had been lying idle in the harbour for two years. He fitted her with sails and masts, renamed her the *Marcella,* and in June 1865 placed her on a freighting route between New Westminster and Puget Sound ports. Next month it was reported in the *British Columbian* that he had made a round trip to Olympia in 13 days.

But there were rumors of gold discoveries in the Big Bend district of the Upper Columbia River north of present-day Revelstoke. Moore was not going to be left out of any gold excitement. Early in 1866 the Colonial government offered a subsidy of $400 a month to anyone who would operate a steamer from Savona, at the foot of Kamloops Lake, to the head of Seymour Arm on Shuswap Lake. From here a 45-mile trail led to the Big Bend diggings.

Moore tendered, but the contract went to his rival, Captain William Irving. He in turn assigned it to the Hudson's Bay Company who built the steamer *Marten* for the route. Undeterred by this setback, Captain Moore took his eldest son, Johnnie, and three men to Shuswap Lake where he built a freight barge. He made a few trips from Savona to Seymour City, but the Big Bend gold rush soon fizzled and Moore was left with the idle barge on his hands.

He then pre-empted land about 12 miles from Kamloops on Kamloops Lake, built a house, purchased five horses and three cows, and sent for his family. Patient Mrs. Moore gathered up her numerous children, the household goods and the inevitable goats, and took passage on Captain Irving's steamer *Onward* to Yale. The household goods and the goats were forwarded to Savona in charge of a teamster, while mother and children crowded into a stagecoach for the bumpy ride through the Fraser Canyon over the Cariboo Wagon Road to Savona. Father was waiting for them with his barge, and family and livestock sailed up Kamloops Lake in fine style to their new home in the wilderness.

They didn't stay long. Farming and cattle raising didn't appeal to

The *Alexandra*, which Captain Moore intended to be the most lavish vessel on the coast. She was one of the few patterned after the twin-funnelled Mississippi River style of vessel, and was "by far the largest sternwheel boat on the northern coast, and when completed as the owners propose will also be the handsomest and most commodious." She was never completely finished because Moore went bankrupt. Her later career was also unsuccessful.

Captain Moore. There was gold in the Cariboo, and where there was gold, that was where he wanted to be. So in the spring of 1866 he barged his family and effects to Savona and set off up the Cariboo Road. His son, Billie, later wrote of this latest move:

"Loading two wagons drawn by two horses each, and with me riding a horse, we started up the road heading for Quesnel. The goats and cows were running loose behind the caravan. My duty was to herd them along, and see that they kept up with the wagons."

On arrival at Quesnel, Captain Moore sold the five horses and the cows and purchased two mules and a new wagon. He moved into the booming gold town of Barkerville where he found work in the mines. Two of the children, Henrietta and Minnie, were sent by stagecoach from Barkerville to a convent in New Westminster. Young Billie, now 12, was considered old enough to go to work.

He was hired out as a shepherd to Van Valkenberg and Harper, who were cattle and sheep raisers. In 1869, J. C. Calbreath, a rancher, contracted for the use of the Moore mule team, and engaged Billie to go to his ranch about 60 miles south of Quesnel to help put in his crops. Years later, Billie commented ruefully:

"Calbreath was a slave driver. He would have worked me even longer hours if the mules could have stood for it."

That year brought reports of another gold strike in the remote Omineca country, so Captain Moore promptly took action. He moved his family and goats to Quesnel where he started to build a barge for he had contracted with a merchant named Ellsmore to deliver 15 tons of freight to Takla Landing on Takla Lake. From here a trail led to the new diggings.

The barge was completed in the early spring of 1870, and after the ice broke up Mrs. Moore and the children were sent to Victoria. It was a sad parting for Mrs. Moore for she had to leave the goats behind. Billie remained to work at Barlow's Store in Quesnel, while Johnnie accompanied his father and a crew of hired men on the back-breaking job of hauling the loaded barge to Takla Landing.

This ordeal entailed towing the craft with long ropes along the river banks and lake edges up the Fraser River via the Cottonwood and Fort George Canyons to Fort George, then up the Nechako and Stuart Rivers, Stuart Lake, Tachie River, Trembleur Lake, Middle River and Takla Lake to the Landing. In all the trip covered some 230 miles, most of it up fast-flowing rivers. The incredible task was completed by early summer. After delivering the supplies, the indomitable Moore and his son set out to investigate the Omineca placer diggings.

Indian bridges looked insecure, although this one at Hagwilget near Hazelton has been strengthened with telephone wire. At Tuya River Captain Moore and his sons built their own rather than use the Indian one.

CHAPTER TWO

After crossing the 40-mile divide from Takla Lake to the Omineca River, they descended this sluggish and crooked stream for 70 miles until they located some claims at the mouth of a small creek. These proved of little value so they back-tracked up the Omineca to the terminus of Takla Lake portage.

Here Ellsmore had opened a store with the goods which Captain Moore and his party hauled so laboriously from Quesnel. Prices were high, with flour $1 a pound and bacon $1.50. The miners called Ellsmore "Hog-em," and soon the name Hogem was attached to the new town which had sprung up.

Captain Moore and Johnnie searched for good placer ground, but they were unlucky. Rather than be frozen in by the long winter, they headed for the sea, over 400 wilderness miles away. Returning to Takla Landing they crossed by their barge to the west side of Takla Lake where there was a half-obliterated Indian trail called Frypan Pass. It led 30 miles over the divide to Babine Lake, which is part of the Skeena River system. It was a difficult route over fallen timber. Adding to their troubles, they were short of supplies and winter was approaching. When they finally reached the old Hudson's Bay Company fort on Babine Lake snow was already on the ground.

Thomas Charles, who was in charge of the post, said that food was so scarce he had only 250 pounds of flour for himself and family for the winter. However, he agreed to sell Captain Moore 50 pounds for $50, which was divided among the six men in the party. From the fort they proceeded down the lake 15 miles to its foot where there was a 75-mile portage by Indian trail to Hazelton on the Skeena River.

Here two pioneers, Cunningham and Rankin, had a trading post where Moore was able to buy provisions. He also procured an Indian canoe in which the party descended 180 miles of the turbulent Skeena River to the Indian village of Spokshute near its mouth. Then the Captain and his son travelled in relative comfort on the *Otter* to Victoria. Here he enjoyed Christmas with his family, with only Billie absent. He was still working in the store at Quesnel.

Never one to squander an idle hour, Bill Moore spent the spring of 1871 at Victoria building a large flat-bottom centreboard schooner called the *Minnie*. He had contracted with a man named Stirling to deliver freight to Takla Landing, and planned to use the *Minnie* to transport the outfit from Victoria to Hazelton. He loaded the vessel with supplies for the Omineca gold diggings and with sons Johnnie and Henry, the latter only 11, sailed up the coast to Woodcock's Landing near the mouth of the Skeena.

Here a man named Woodcock had a store and stopping place. From him, Captain Moore learned that the provincial government had awarded a contract to Cunningham and Hankin to build a pack trail over the Skeena portage from Hazelton to Babine Lake and that Woodcock was a sub-contractor. Never one to be left out of the action, the Captain made a deal to supply the transportation to the site. A herd of mules was added to the *Minnie's* cargo, plus a crew of 30 men to build the trail.

But the task of ascending the Skeena with a loaded barge was beyond even Captain Moore's herculean powers. At the canyon of the Skeena the trail crew deserted him and went on by foot. That left the doughty captain in desperate straits. His hay was gone, his food low and he had only 30 sacks of grain left between the mules and starvation. He tethered the mules on the shore in two feet of snow and sent Johnnie down-river to recruit a crew of Indians.

Then he tried again, but the *Minnie* was quite hopeless in the Skeena shallows and he had to leave her behind. He and the boys drove the mules along the bank for 90 miles, and when they reached Hazelton had lost only one animal. The others were in prime condition to work on the Babine trail which had already been surveyed by Edgar Dewdney. The 60-mile trail was completed that summer.

Captain Moore and his boys meanwhile proceeded over the Frypan Pass to Takla Lake where he had arranged to meet his son, Billie. The latter followed the water route from Quesnel and arrived at Frypan Landing to find his father and brothers repairing the barge they had cached there the previous year. The freight which Moore had contracted to deliver to Takla Landing was packed from Hazelton on the backs of Indians and delivered across the lake by the barge.

At Takla Landing they met a man who had started from Quesnel with 56 pack animals but wore them out by the time he reached the lower end of Trembleur Lake. He engaged Captain Moore to take his barge down Trembleur Lake, pick up the freight the animals were carrying and 30 of the mules for delivery at Takla Landing. Moore purchased the remaining 26 for $200 per head, including their saddles and trappings.

He left his two younger sons, Billie and Henry, and two other men with instructions to drive the mules along the river and lake to a point opposite Frypan Landing. The boys made the rendezvous but Captain Moore missed their signals. As a result they were four days without food. When their father finally found them he kissed them both, with tears running down his cheeks, for the rugged old frontiersman dearly loved his family.

Captain Moore barged the mules across Takla Lake to Frypan Landing, and from there herded them to Babine Lake where Woodcock with a crew of men had the Skeena Portage trail well under way. Moore employed his 26 mules packing on the trail. At the approach of winter they were taken 40 miles down the Skeena by two men who were detailed to look after them until spring.

Captain Moore, meanwhile, had recovered the barge *Minnie*, and he and his three boys, with 50 miners, started down-river, covering 150 miles in less than two days. At Woodcock's Landing they took passage on the *Otter* for Victoria. That winter the ever optimistic Moore made a contract with the Hudson's Bay Company to freight supplies for them up the Skeena in the spring.

Again with his three sons, he took passage in the *Otter* in March 1872. He disembarked at Spokshute, which had been renamed Port Essington by Robert Cunningham, who had moved from Hazelton. Here Captain Moore hired some extra men and started to build two barges of 15 tons capacity, each suitable for freighting up the river. When they were completed, he hired 12 natives to man each barge and 12 more to handle two large canoes. The captain was in charge of the lead barge; Johnnie, the second;

Most interior B.C. rivers are fast-flowing and laced with sections of white-water canyons. As a consequence, moving supplies by flat-bottomed scows was dangerous and brutal work. Downstream, crews usually ran rapids, but upstream spent hours and even days in the cold water, pulling and prying the cumbersome craft foot by foot. Captain Moore never flinched from danger, challenging as necessary the Fraser, Nechako, Stuart, Skeena, Stikine and Yukon Rivers.

while Billie brought up the rear in the canoes.

"On reaching the Kitselas canyon," Billie later wrote, "long lines were passed from the leading barge to the other barge, and to the canoes trailing behind, all in line. A long rope was taken ashore and anchored as far ahead as it would reach. The first barge had a capstan installation, with which to pull the barges through the rapids and canyons. When the first barge had been pulled up as far as possible it would be anchored to the shore, the other barges and canoes pulled up to this point; then the line would be taken ahead, and the process repeated until the barges and canoes had all passed through the canyon. This procedure was necessary many times before we had completed the trip up the Skeena. There were stretches where the current was not so swift, and then we would tow the barge with shore lines."

A short distance above Kitselas they were met by a canoe with Tom Hankin aboard. He warned them that the Indians at Kitsequekla — a tribe called the Sticks — were hostile and that several shots had been fired upon him as he passed through the canyon. Earlier some careless miners had accidentally burned down the Indians' winter village and the tribesmen were out for vengeance.

Despite this warning, Moore and his sons decided to continue on their way. On their arrival at Kitsequekla Canyon they saw 60 or 70 natives sitting with their blankets around them, not a woman or child in sight. Moore's coast natives, who were composed of Haida, Tongass and Tsimpseans, warned him that he and his sons were liable to get killed, and so were they since the Sticks didn't like the coast natives either.

Moore told his crew that they must stand by him, and that the Hudson's Bay Company would pay them to take care of their goods. The natives said they could do nothing without guns, so Moore ordered them to open four cases of muskets and ammunition and arm themselves. In addition, Moore and his sons had two Henry rifles and two revolvers. When they got abreast of the village, two natives said: "We will not let you go up unless you pay."

Moore answered that he could not since the goods didn't belong to him, but that he was sure the government would pay for their lost village.

The Sticks answered: "If you try to go farther we will fight."

Moore warned them that if they harmed him or his crew, three of their chiefs who had gone to the coast would not be allowed to return. He then ordered his crew to proceed. During the two days it took to heave the barges through the canyon armed Sticks watched them, but the threat of reprisal kept the natives from attacking.

Despite the threat the flotilla arrived at Hazelton with the goods intact. The mules were in good shape and were quickly

An unknown sternwheeler at Telegraph Creek in the 1880s. The community was the gateway to the Cassiar wilderness where Captain Moore and his sons discovered gold and took out a fortune of some $80,000.

The photo below shows the rugged Cassiar country. The Moores were three days towing and poling their raft of supplies down 24-mile-long Dease Lake. In all, they were 62 days boating and back-packing their supplies 260 miles from Fort Wrangell.

loaded with freight and started over the Babine trail in charge of Johnnie. Then Captain Moore and his two younger sons returned down the Skeena for another load. As they passed through Kitsequekla several shots were fired at them, one hitting the leg of a crew member. Another struck the steering oar six inches from Captain Moore's hand. One of the crew grabbed Moore's rifle and fired several shots in return but since the river was rising very rapidly because of the spring freshet, it took all their attention to manage the barges.

On their arrival at the mouth of the river they found that the Government, hearing of the Indian trouble, had sent up a gunboat — HMS *Scout* — with Lieutenant-Governor J. W. Trutch. He met the chiefs from the Stick tribe, explained that their misfortune was the result of an accident, and distributed $600 as recompense.

The next trip up the river Captain Moore observed that there was not a native in sight at Kitsequekla. They had heard of the man-of-war at Port Essington and had taken their families back into the woods. After the chiefs returned to their homes there were no more threats.

Captain Moore made three trips to Hazelton that season. Then with winter drawing near he arranged for Johnnie to drive the mules over the Indian "grease" trail from the Skeena to the Nass River. Captain Moore and his younger sons took the barges down to Port Essington and transferred to the *Minnie*. They then sailed the schooner up to the Nass River where they picked up Johnnie with 24 mules, two having been killed by Kitwanga Indians who had demanded payment for the use of the trail.

The *Minnie* proceeded down Observatory Inlet and two days later anchored in a lagoon about 15 miles south of Woodcock's Landing. Captain Moore had picked the location — still called Moore Cove — to winter the pack animals. Here they were unloaded and left in the care of the three boys and a negro cook, Eli Harrison.

The boys built a 20- x 30-foot cabin, and according to Billie, they gained weight and enjoyed "the life of Riley" that winter. The same could not be said for the mules. There was so much snow and ice on the flats they all died of starvation.

In March the boys received a letter from their father instructing them to put the schooner and a barge in shape. A new gold strike had been reported the previous season by prospectors Thibert and McCullough on the bars of Delure Creek in the Cassiar district. Needless to say, Captain Moore was determined to be in the vanguard that spring.

He met his sons at Port Essington with a large supply of provisions which were loaded aboard the *Minnie.* With the barge in tow the family set sail for Fort Wrangell, about 200 miles north, where they arrived on April 4. The *Otter* had just landed a large cargo for the Hudson's Bay post about 75 miles up the Stikine River, and veteran prospector Buck Choquette was supervising loading of the goods into native canoes.

The Moore family pulled the *Minnie* up on a beach and left her in charge of an Indian chief, while they prepared the barge with oars, sails and poles for a voyage up the Stikine. Six prospectors and two hired Indian helpers joined the party in addition to Moore and his three sons. They left Wrangell on April 20, but when they reached the H.B.C. post there was still four to six feet of snow along the river bank. Because of the snow and rugged terrain they were three days lining through Stikine Canyon, although once at the upper end conditions greatly improved since they had passed through the Coast Mountains into the Interior dry belt.

The *Inlander* entering Kitselas Canyon on the Skeena River, one of many treacherous sections on the 180 miles from Spokshute to Hazelton. Captain Moore and his crew fought their way upstream with two, 15-ton barges, each pulled by hand. An additional hazard was Indians who threatened to kill Moore and did shoot one of his crew. The Captain refused to be intimidated and continued the slow progress upstream. Unfortunately, on Vancouver Island in 1885 Indians did murder Moore's son, Henry, and three shipmates. Henry had a wife and four young children.

In all, the Captain and his party were 12 days fighting the barge up the river with poles, oars, sails and towline to Telegraph Creek, 150 miles from Wrangell and the head of navigation on the Stikine. From Telegraph Creek they had to backpack their goods, a brutal undertaking. Each man packed until he was tired, then cached his pack and returned for another load. This process was repeated day in and day out, from sunrise to sunset, a continual trek of back-breaking drudgery.

The trail followed the right bank of the river, a roller-coaster affair with a number of precipitous gulches. In places it clung to the side of a steep mountain where a slip meant tumbling into the river below. About 15 miles from Telegraph Creek it crossed the Tahtlan River over an Indian bridge that consisted of poles bound together by withes without nails. The suspension span was about

75 feet long and most insecure. Ten miles further along the party came to the Tuya River, also crossed by a 42-foot Indian bridge. Since it looked even more rickety than the Tahtlan span they spent four days building a bridge of their own.

The trail from there led through comparatively open country and gave the appearance of easy going. But the route proved tough for walking, being of a swampy nature carpeted with moss and laced with obstacles such as fallen timber and scrub bush. Since Henry was only 14 years old, his father and brothers thought his loads too heavy for him. He insisted on carrying as much as the others, even though one of his packs consisted of a long whipsaw and other awkward tools. The party made about 5 miles progress each day. With the relay of packs, this meant they were walking about 20 miles a day, wet to the waist from crossing many streams and wading through swamps.

Twenty-eight days after leaving Miller's post on the Stikine the weary men reached the shore of Dease Lake. Here they cached their goods and after only a day of rest started back. They travelled light, taking only enough food for three days and no blankets, and arrived at Miller's on the morning of the third day from Dease Lake.

"All we did that day was to prepare two packs for each man, and then we rested the remainder of the time," Billie later recalled.

There was some doubt, however, about the extent of the "rest." The Indians in the party wanted to quit, but Miller, who could speak their language, persuaded them to complete their contract. Next day, accompanied by some other prospectors who had come up from the Coast, the party again set out for Dease Lake.

On their arrival at Tuya River they met about 15 Stick Indians and their families who said that they would not let the whites go any farther as they would scare the game away. The whites deliberately began to load their firearms. This action frightened the natives, who pointed to their wives and children and demanded payment for using their trails and bridges. Captain Moore agreed to give them $20 and provisions for their supper, so friendly relations were reached.

They reached Dease Lake in 20 days from Miller's post, and proceeded to build a raft to transport their goods down the lake. The two Indians were paid $50 each and returned to the Coast taking letters for Mrs. Moore in Victoria. Poling and towing along the shore, the party took three days to reach the foot of the lake, a distance of 24 miles. They had spent 62 days of the most gruelling work, boating and packing their supplies and gear the 260 miles from Fort Wrangell.

They camped at the mouth of a small creek, now known as Thibert Creek, where they found a new boat and evidence of a camp. Proceeding 4 miles up the creek they met Henry Thibert and his partners. They had two rockers in operation and were taking out three to six ounces of gold a day per man, worth $50 to $100. The new arrivals then proceeded to stake claims.

The ground was frozen hard under the moss and it took so much time to thaw the party could make only $6 to $8 a day. Johnnie and Billie were dissatisfied, and, against the advice of their father, moved 12 miles up the lake to a creek called Dease they had passed on the way down. When they got 3 miles upstream they found gold in the first pan. Soon gold was running 10 to 50 cents in every pan and the entire party from Thibert Creek moved to the new diggings.

Captain Moore and his three boys each located a discovery claim, 600 feet for the four of them. Although Henry was under age, the miners voted that he could hold a claim. This decision was later upheld in special legislation passed by the Provincial Government at Victoria.

Captain Moore and his sons were cleaning up about $70 a day when the father was taken seriously ill. It was likely scurvy, for one of Thibert's party died of scurvy at this time. Moore insisted on continuing at the job but his sons finally compelled him to quit as he was failing fast. They made him a comfortable bed and Henry stayed in camp to look after him. They shot a few grouse and caught some fish, and with this change of diet the sturdy old captain began to improve.

By September 18 they had cleaned up $5,000 and decided to leave since there was already six inches of snow on the ground. They left their tools and utensils in a cache and set out for Telegraph Creek, carrying only a blanket apiece and the remains of their provisions: 25 pounds of flour, a small slab of bacon and a little sugar. Because of these scanty supplies, their diet on the three-day hike consisted mainly of hot cakes.

At Miller's they refloated their barge and in a few days were on their way down the river to Fort Wrangell where they caught the Alaska mail steamer *California* to Victoria. It was a great relief to Mrs. Moore once more to have her brood under her roof.

The household that winter was full of glorious talk of the wealth to be won from placer claims on Dease Creek. Captain Moore was once more a man of substance, no longer the discredited bankrupt of 1865. He convinced the British Columbia Government that a good pack trail from Telegraph Creek to Dease Lake was a necessity and that he was the man to do the job. He was awarded a contract in partnership with Morris Lenz, a Victoria merchant, to build a trail and operate a pack train. The Captain was back in the transportation business.

CHAPTER THREE

Dease Town, or Laketon as it was later known, was booming. "Many claims were paying well, and money was everywhere," Billie Moore recalled. "There were several stores, and dance halls filled mostly with native girls from the coast. Saloons and all kinds of gambling were going on. Judge Sullivan, who was the gold com-

The *Western Slope* which Captain Moore operated with one safety valve set to read low and the other jammed shut with a block of wood.

missioner, was busy holding court, principally on mining disputes. There was no gun play and no one expected any, as the law was carried out very fast in British Columbia."

By autumn there were about 4,500 white men, 300 Chinese and 50 negroes in the Cassiar district. A new strike was made at Mc-Dame Creek, about 150 miles down the Dease River, and there was a stampede to the digging.

The Moore boys, meanwhile were busy working their claims on Dease Creek, and by the end of the season had accumulated close

to $50,000, a large fortune in these days. They met their father and all went down the Stikine to Fort Wrangell. The former sleepy village of three white inhabitants was now riding high on the crest of the gold boom, with saloons, gambling dens and dance halls running full blast. Before leaving Fort Wrangell for his Victoria home, Captain Moore arranged for a crew to cut cedar for construction of a new sternwheeler he planned for the Stikine River.

This new vessel was launched in Victoria on March 22, 1875. She was the *Gertrude*, 120 feet long and fitted with 10 water-tight compartments. To keep her draft shallow the Captain had specified that everything be made in the lightest but most substantial manner. With her the Captain was once more in his favorite occupation — a ship owner. Unfortunately, before long he would again be bankrupt.

The *Gertrude* left Victoria for Fort Wrangell on April 15, 1875, and immediately entered the booming Stikine River trade with Captain Bill Moore in the pilothouse. Billie joined his father after a brief spell of schooling at Oakland, while young Ben, now 10, got his introduction to steamboating on the river. Johnnie, or "J.W.," as he was generally called, operated the placer claims in the Cassiar.

On her first trip up the river the *Gertrude* was loaded to capacity with passengers, 50 horses and general cargo. She managed to reach Telegraph Creek, the highest point any steamer had yet navigated and was acclaimed a "lightning-striker."

Three steamboats operated on the Stikine that summer, but Captain Moore soon disposed of the opposition. The *Hope*, under Captain Otis Parsons, made only two trips in the season. Her machinery and boiler were removed and she was converted into a floating boarding house at Wrangell. An arrangement was made with Captain John Irving's *Glenora* to keep up the rates, and later Moore bought the vessel.

Ben Moore subsequently wrote nostalgically of his happy life on the Stikine that prosperous year of 1875:

"The *Gertrude* used to take the least time of any of the steamers on the river. The other boats would be often stuck on the bars, and at other times with lines out with a dozen men on the capstan heaving them over the bars and engines working full power, while our boat would walk right by them; and sometimes we would sound the whistle and shake a line over the stern at them as we passed by.

"This steamer, *Gertrude*, was certainly my father's pet boat out of the numerous steamers he owned both before and after her time, and I and all our family loved this grand little steamer, to say nothing of endless praises spoken of her by all who travelled on her. Those were our balmy days too. Our family were all together, and we were young."

He described the Stikine as a "very swift stream with many snags and shifting bars, the latter necessitating the picking out of new channels every trip. And if a boat should run heavily aground on a downstream trip ... especially toward the fall of the year when the water is falling permanently ... it would mean perhaps a total loss of the vessel, for if she could not be backed off the bar she would be frozen in for the winter and then, in the spring break-up, be demolished by the ice."

J. W. Moore returned from the Cassiar claims late in October with a good season's clean-up. Things now looked very promising for the Moore family. After assisting Captain Irving to put up the *Glenora* for the winter, Captain Bill Moore took the *Gertrude* to the Fraser, where he ran cut-rate opposition to John Irving's *Royal City* for a few weeks.

He could never resist a rate war, even if it cost him money, and even if it hurt an old friend of the family like Irving. This flaw in Moore's character was to cause him much grief and eventually break him. He forced the fare from New Westminster to Yale down to $1, then gave up the battle and laid up the *Gertrude* at Victoria for the winter.

Captain Moore's ambitions now expanded. With the wealth of the Cassiar mines and his steamboat profits, he set out on a program of expansion. He purchased a retired British gunboat, the *Grappler*, which had been converted to a coastwise freighter and put her to sea under command of Captain William Meyer, who had married his daughter, Henrietta.

During the winter of 1875-76 the *Grappler* ran on the B.C. coast, towing logs and sailing vessels. Captain Moore also purchased five waterfront lots in Victoria's Inner Harbour and built a large house plus ways for ship repairing. He also purchased the *Glenora* from Captain Irving with the understanding that Irving would not interest himself in any other steamer on the Stikine River.

During the 1876 season Captain Moore flourished as a steamboat magnate. The *Grappler* was kept busy hauling supplies from Victoria to Fort Wrangell where they were trans-shipped for the Cassiar mines aboard the *Gertrude* and the *Glenora*. He skippered the *Gertrude* and Billie commanded the *Glenora*.

Billie had developed into a natural riverboatman and soon became the best navigator on the Stikine, a reputation he later took to the Fraser and Yukon Rivers. Son J. W., meanwhile, was kept busy working the family claims at Dease Creek. But the gold had become increasingly marginal and at the end of the 1876 season he sold out to a Chinese syndicate. The *Gertrude* was laid up that winter at Glenora.

With the opening of navigation in 1877 Captain Moore couldn't resist bringing the *Gertrude* to the Fraser River to run in opposition

A direct link with the flamboyant sternwheel era on the Fraser River is Irving House in New Westminster, built between 1862-64 by Captain John Irving. Bought by the city of New Westminster, today it is an historic center, open to the public and reflecting almost unchanged the life style of the 1860s.

The *Reliance*, below, was launched by Captain Irving in 1876. Captain Moore realized that she would be tough competition and "had a meeting" with Irving. Thereafter, Moore agreed to stay on the Stikine River. But he soon returned to the Fraser River with the *Western Slope* and promptly started one of his many rate wars with Irving.

to Captain Irving. The steamers raced up and down the Fraser, each trying to win the speed record. Moore proudly advertised that the *Gertrude* was making the 110-mile passage to Yale in 10 hours running time, and was coming downstream in only 5. Captain Irving's *Reliance* countered with a record of 9 hours up the river. Opposition by the *Gertrude* was brief and unprofitable, and Captain Moore soon had her back on the Stikine in time to take the first consignment of passengers and freight from the *Grappler* up to Telegraph Creek. The brief period of opposition on the Fraser had merely been a token defiance from Captain Moore to his young rival, John Irving.

The year 1878 was also reasonably profitable on the Stikine route, despite the arrival of further competition, the Puget Sound sternwheeler *Nellie.* It was owned by J. C. Calbreath, packer and storekeeper, who in 1862 had introduced camels into British Columbia for packing to the Cariboo goldfield.

Flushed with success, Captain Moore repeated the same mistake he had made years before when he built the *Alexandra.* He ordered a boat that was too big and expensive for the dwindling business. His idea was to build a sternwheeler sufficiently seaworthy to take over the coastwise route of the *Grappler* and ascend the Stikine River beyond the Alaska-B.C. boundary to trans-ship passengers and cargo to the *Gertrude.*

The powerful new sternwheeler was the 156-foot-long *Western Slope,* launched at Victoria on May 8, 1879. Captain Moore spared no expense in her construction; in fact, he over-extended himself. The Cassiar gold operations no longer yielded treasure and during the season with competition keen everywhere the Captain lost money.

Things were worse in 1880. During a dense fog the *Grappler* ran on a reef and sank, her cargo of grain and hay a total loss. Moore had no insurance and though he raised the vessel at great cost, he was forced to sell her. With the opening of navigation on the Fraser River in early April he embarked on a project that had occupied his mind since the days of the ill-fated *Alexandra* — the operation of a through steamer from Victoria to Yale. The move meant strong competition with Captain John Irving's well entrenched Pioneer Line, but Moore could never resist the chance for a steamboat war. He called his new enterprise the People's Steamboat Line.

On April 3, 1880, the *Victoria Colonist* carried an advertisement for the new line which read, in part:

"The Swift, Commodious and Elegantly Appointed Sternwheel Steamer *Western Slope,* Captain Wm. Moore, Will resume her Regular Trips from Victoria to New Westm'ster, Riverside, Chilliwhack, Ft. Hope, Emory City & Yale, on Wednesday, April 14th. The Splendid Light Draft, Fast and Powerful Steamboat *Gertrude* will make

Regular Trips during the Season from New Westminster to Yale and Intermediate Ports."

In a slap at Captain John Irving's opposition service, the advertisement also noted that the "People's Steamboat Line is the only Line that carries Passengers from Victoria through to the Head of Steamboat Navigation on Fraser River without detention at New Westminster or change of boats. Passengers travelling by any other line must remain at New Westminster from 3 o'clock in the afternoon till 7 o'clock the following morning at heavy expense for hotel accommodation, etc. Freight shipped by any other line must be trans-shipped at New Westminster, pay wharfage there, and run the risk of damage by double handling."

Captain Irving countered by warning that "Passengers by any other Line will have to remain overnight tied up in the midst of an impenetrable forest, with nothing to relieve the tedium of the weary hours but a constant warfare with the bloodthirsty mosquito, and will be forced to put up with accommodations of an inferior class.

"In contrast," the advertisement continued, "passengers from Victoria travelling by this Line will have an opportunity of seeing New Westminster and visiting and inspecting the handsome and important Public Buildings and other objects of interest located there, and will arrive at their destination about the same time as if they had proceeded up stream the same day that they arrived at New Westminster."

It may have been the mosquitoes, or perhaps the "accommodations of an inferior class," but after a few weeks of furious competition Captain Moore again faced financial disaster. He sank the last of his savings into the venture, but to no avail. In June his

From 1858 to completion of the CPR in 1886, sternwheel steamers were vital links in the pioneer transportation system, with Yale the gateway to Interior B.C. for nearly 30 years. Passengers arrived by sternwheeler and transferred to stagecoaches for the 400-mile trip northward to Barkerville, while freight went into wagons, opposite, drawn by oxen, horses or mules. Because 10 miles a day was good progress with oxen, the trek northward to Barkerville took up to two months.

creditors held a meeting to consider selling the *Western Slope*. He managed to stave off disaster by chartering the vessel to his old rival, Captain Irving, who had a contract to move thousands of tons of rails to Yale for a massive new construction project, the Canadian Pacific Railway. Moore sent the *Gertrude* back to the Stikine, but the Cassiar boom was nearly over and she ran at a loss during the brief season.

Construction of the C.P.R. brought prosperity to the Fraser River in 1881 and provided a temporary respite for Captain Moore from his creditors. He was again in the fray, running the *Western Slope* once more in opposition to Captain Irving. The *Western Slope* offered direct sailings twice a week between Victoria and Yale.

There was lots of excitement, for Andrew Onderdonk, contractor for the railway through the Fraser and Thompson River Canyons to Savona, was bringing in thousands of Chinese coolies to work on construction. In addition, his agents hired the scrapings of the San Francisco waterfront, who were brought up by direct steamer to Victoria or New Westminster. They soon won the sarcastic nickname "Onderdonk's Lambs."

An item in the New Westminster *Dominion Pacific Herald* on June 1, 1881, gives an amusing glimpse of Captain William Moore's rather high-handed steamboating operations:

"Owing to the number of dead-beats recently assaying to come down from Yale on the steamers, Capt. Moore has adopted the precaution of collecting fare from suspicious looking cases before casting off. Last Monday morning, in going the usual rounds, in the performance of this duty, the Captain came across a Chinaman in a sitting posture, with his blanket round him. Upon applying for his fare and receiving no response, the impatient Captain gave

'John' a lively punch, supposing he was asleep, which caused him to tumble over.

"Upon examination, he was found to be dead. It appears that the dead Chinaman had been placed on the steamer in that posture during the night by his countrymen, with the idea of getting a free passage to Victoria. Capt. Moore could not see it in that light, and the dead-head was unceremoniously deposited on the beach at Yale, where he still lay ... at 10 o'clock on Monday."

Another aspect of Captain Moore's steamboat operation was that he didn't pay much attention to regulations. In particular, he tended to ignore one that limited steam pressure to 100 pounds. He claimed he could take the *Western Slope* through Sawmill Riffle, below Yale, with 89 pounds 2½ ounces of stream. This statement caused the New Westminster paper to comment: "Some inclined that either the Captain or the steam-gauge lied."

During this period of intense competition the *Herald* did its best to discredit Captain Moore, for he was a resident of Victoria, while Captain Irving was the pride of New Westminster. Furthermore, Moore had the temerity to offer through service from Victoria to Yale without trans-shipment at New Westminster.

The paper soon had an opportunity to attack Moore, who had quarrelled with his second engineer and kicked him off the *Western Slope*. The engineer retaliated by laying an information that Moore was exceeding the 100-pound limit of steam pressure. The case was heard in New Westminster police court and received maximum publicity. The discharged engineer testified that not one safety valve on the *Western Slope* worked and that the boiler was burned out. The captain gave standing orders to carry 110 pounds of steam, but the vessel more frequently carried up to 140 pounds. A fireman testified:

"One valve was wedged down so that it could not possibly work; the other stood at 140 pounds and I never knew it to blow off!"

Captain Irving testified that he had noticed a difference of 30 pounds in the ship's two steam gauges. Captain George Odin testified that the *Western Slope* could not reach Yale with less than 140 pounds. The result was that Captain Moore and his Chief Engineer were each fined $200 by the magistrate.

The Victoria *Colonist* screamed with anger at the verdict, which it called a persecution and a conspiracy. It promptly started a public subscription to pay the fines, thus "setting the law at open and utter defiance," as the *Herald* put it. There was an echo of the affair a few weeks later when the New Westminster paper, still smarting with righteous disapproval, commented:

"The steamer *Western Slope* has certainly enjoyed a remarkable run of success during the greater part of the season ... coming and

FRASER RIVER
PIONEER LINE OF STEAMERS.
THE ONLY REGULAR AND OLD RELIABLE LINE.

A STEAMER OF THIS LINE WILL LEAVE NEW WESTMINSTER FOR

HOPE, EMORY, YALE & WAY PORTS

After the arrival of the Hudson Bay Company's Steamers from Victoria, Carrying H. M. Mails, the B. C. Express, and Freight and Passengers.

THROUGH TICKETS to any point on the route may be had on application to the Hudson Bay Co., Victoria.

PASSENGERS FOR SKAGET, YALE, EMORY AND OTHER PLACES

Will find it to their advantage to travel by these well known and popular lines which offer the best accommodation, perfect regularity, great speed and
LOW RATES.

PASSENGERS from Victoria travelling by this Line will have an opportunity of seeing New Westminster and visiting and inspecting the handsome and important Public Buildings and other objects of interest located there, and will arrive at their destination about the same time as if they had proceeded up stream the same day that they arrived at New Westminster.

Passengers by any other Line will have to remain overnight tied up in the midst of an impenetrable forest, with nothing to relieve the tedium of the weary hours but a constant warfare with the bloodthirsty mosquito, and will be forced to put up with accommodations of an inferior class.

For particulars or rates apply at the HUDSON BAY CO.'S OFFICE, VICTORIA, or at Office of the PIONEER LINE, NEW WESTMINSTER.

JOHN IRVING, Manager Pioneer Line.

Victoria, April 20, 1880. ap20

THE PEOPLE'S
STEAMBOAT LINE.

The Swift, Commodious and Elegantly Appointed Sternwheel Steamer

WESTERN SLOPE,

(831 TONS GROSS REGISTER.) CAPTAIN WM. MOORE,

Will resume her Regular Trips from Victoria to

NEW WESTM'STER, RIVERSIDE, CHILLIWHACK, FT. HOPE
EMORY CITY & YALE,
ON WEDNESDAY, APRIL 14TH.

The Splendid Light Draft, Fast and Powerful Steamboat

GERTRUDE,

(301 Tons Gross Register) will make Regular Trips during the Season from New Westminster to Yale and Intermediate Ports.

THE PEOPLE'S STEAMBOAT LINE is the only Line that carries Passengers from Victoria through to the Head of Steamboat Navigation on Fraser River WITHOUT DETENTION AT NEW WESTMINSTER OR CHANGE OF BOATS.

PASSENGERS traveling by any other line must remain at New Westminster from 3 o'clock in the afternoon till 7 o'clock the following morning at heavy expense for hotel accommodation, etc.

FREIGHT shipped by any other line must be transhipped at New Westminster, pay wharfage there, and run the risk of damage by double handling.

Agent at Victoria, J. W. MOORE, with whom Contracts may be made and Through Tickets sold. ap3 going with a degree of regularity that shames some other boats, and sailing through Dominion statutes with as much assurance as she would run over a luckless fisherman's net."

To meet the competition of the *Western Slope,* Captain Irving ordered a new 167-foot sternwheeler designed to run between Victoria and Yale. She was the *Elizabeth J. Irving,* biggest paddle-wheeler yet to appear on the Fraser. She was a marvel of the age for she carried an electric searchlight on her pilothouse, and it was claimed she would run during the dark hours.

The arrival of the newcomer naturally called for a race with the *Western Slope,* which occurred on the *Elizabeth J. Irving's* second voyage up-river on September 29, 1881. Captain Bill Moore's youngest son, Ben, later described the event:

"It was about a standoff for speed between the *Elizabeth J. Irving* and our boat," he wrote. "We had been racing a little after leaving New Westminster, and Irving's boat made a landing at Chilliwack about sixty miles up-river. We landed a few moments later, putting our bows into the mud bank just inside of her fan tail. After a little, Irving's boat pulled out and started out upriver. This was only her second trip. She was a brand-new elegant boat. Capt. Irving himself was on board. They tooted their whistle at us, and someone on board of her shook a hawser over her stern at us just as we pulled out immediately after them.

"Well, it was quite a race all day long, nip and tuck; but the *Irving* did keep just about a mile or two ahead of us. We could not pass her, and the distance between the two vessels varied but little. At last we neared Fort Hope Bend where there is a sharp turn or elbow in the river with a bluff rocky point on the right, and which at certain stages of the river is exceedingly difficult ... especially for a heavily built boat such as the *Slope* was ... to make this turn.

"I was aboard our boat in the pilothouse with three men at the big double wheel. We made three attempts to round this curve, and had the steamer turn round and look at us three times and drift downstream a couple of miles, and on the fourth attempt got through. The *Irving,* of course, got out of sight, having made the turn around the point successfully. But we did not know, of course, whether she intended to make a landing at Fort Hope, or continue on through to Yale, fifteen miles farther on.

"My father and brother William, myself, and my brother Henry were in the pilothouse, too, all four of us at the wheel (we had no steam steering-gear on our boat then), when all at once we noticed through the trees and an opening over the point a large mass of smoke rising high up in the air which we all at the first moment thought was a slab-pile fire at the Fort Hope Sawmill.

"At this point we had just gotten to within a short distance of the critical curve or bend referred to, when I spied a smokestack in the middle of the huge mass of smoke.

"Oh, it is the *Elizabeth Irving* on fire!" I cried aloud.

"A moment later this magnificent brand-new steamer, which cost her owner some eighty thousand dollars, was a mass of flames from stern to stern and came bearing down on us with her wheel slowly turning, head on downstream just as though still being steered by her pilot.

"We were in imminent danger. Immediately reversing our engines, we drifted back downstream out of the way of this floating mass of flames and smoke, but we could already feel the heat of it all. It was an extraordinary sight to see the way the boat came around the bend, downstream with her engines slowly turning over the wheel.

"By this time we had gotten well out of danger, and very soon the burning vessel grounded on a bar perhaps five miles below Fort Hope Bend, where she burned up completely and nothing was left but the charred shell of the hull."

Ben Moore gives an account of a second adventurous voyage of the *Western Slope* that busy summer:

"On another occasion on a trip down from Fort Yale, I was aboard the *Western Slope*. We used to leave Yale during the summer months at about 3 or 4 a.m., when it began to be fairly good daylight, and used to arrive at Victoria by 3.30 or 4 p.m. on the same day.

"About fifteen miles below Yale there are two huge rocks towering high up. The river along there runs very swiftly and great care and experience are required in handling a large heavy boat like the *Slope* in making the shootdown through the Sisters. This trip she took a shear on us and struck a sunken rock. I rushed down to the fireroom to see if any water was showing up in the hold. When I got there I saw at once that the boat was already leaking heavily, for chips and bark and small sticks were afloat in the fireroom.

"I sent word to the pilothouse and we headed her for the nearest shore, where she lay for a while with her nose on the beach while we built a coffer dam around the hole in the vessel's bottom which, fortunately, was in the fireroom and away from the boilers where we could work at it. After a few hours we proceeded on our trip through to Victoria.

"Emory's Bar used to be a hard place for steamers. The water was very shallow here at times, and swift. Often the boats would stand still with a full head of steam on, trying to head upstream, and one could hear the loud coughing of their exhausts through the funnels for miles; and at times cinders as large as your hand would shoot up in the air and mingle with flame and smoke."

CHAPTER FOUR

Business on the Fraser was so brisk in 1881 that Captain Moore staved off the most pressing of his creditors. However, things continued to slacken on the Stikine River, so early in 1882 he sold the *Gertrude* to Calbreath, Grant and Cook, the Cassiar merchants. Then he built another steamer at Victoria for the Fraser River, a 90-foot shallow draft sternwheeler *Pacific Slope*. She was designed to act as consort to the *Western Slope*, which at low water couldn't get up as far as Yale. Goods and passengers were trans-shipped at Murderer's Bar below Hope to the smaller vessel, which then completed the upriver journey.

Before the year was over, however, Captain Moore's financial problems forced him to sell the *Pacific Slope* to Andrew Onderdonk, the contractor building the C.P.R. railway through the Fraser Can-

"Skookum Jim," the Indian with whom Captain Moore discovered the White Pass, main entry point to the Yukon. In 1896 Skookum Jim was a co-discoverer of the gold which started the Klondike stampede.

William Ogilvie, the Canadian Government surveyor for whom Captain Moore worked in 1887. The Captain was in charge of packing supplies into the Yukon and had to build and navigate a barge down the Yukon River, a formidable assignment for a man of 65. He not only completed these duties but also explored a 45-mile route through the Coast Mountains which Ogilvie named the White Pass.

yon. Under the name *Myra*, he used her for carrying construction supplies. By the end of 1882, Moore was again adjudged a bankrupt.

All of his hard-won wealth from the Cassiar mines was gone and his pioneering efforts as a trail blazer were in vain. That sorry winter his creditors seized the *Western Slope* as well as his shipyard, three town lots in Victoria, his two-storey residence, another residence occupied by his son-in-law, Captain Meyer, their furniture, and an accumulation of machinery. He was now over 60 years old, had been in B.C. nearly 25 years but was poorer than when he arrived. The situation would have daunted less hardy men, but not Captain Moore.

On January 9, 1883, Captain John Irving bought the *Western Slope* at a sheriff's sale in Victoria for only $16,500. This gave him a monopoly of the Fraser River trade, for he had also purchased the *Gertrude* and was about to amalgamate his steamers with those of

Miles Canyon on the Yukon River. This Canyon and Whitehorse Rapids formed a 3-mile waterway that claimed scores of lives during the Klondike gold rush. Captain Moore and his sons explored the region in 1887. The rugged individualist was then 65, the Klondike gold discovery still 9 years in the future.

the Hudson's Bay Company to form the Canadian Pacific Navigation Co. Ltd.

But Moore was determined to get his revenge on Captain Irving, who was successfully operating the *R.P. Rithet* on a winter schedule between Victoria and New Westminster. He prepared a memorial which he presented to Thomas Westgarth, the steamboat inspector, in which he claimed the *Rithet* was unseaworthy, as opposed to "Steamers of a more substantial class, such as the *Western Slope.*"

Those who signed the memorial made it rather suspect. In addition to Captain Bill Moore, the complaint was signed by three sons, two sons-in-law, the builder of the *Slope,* her chief engineer, the ship's carpenter, the chief mortgage holder, and kindred souls, all of whom had an axe to grind. Westgarth issued an order forbidding the R.P. *Rithet* from crossing the Strait of Georgia during the winter months, and Captain Irving was forced to make a hasty trip to Ottawa where he applied political pressure to get the order countermanded.

Captain Irving, however, was not a man to nurse a grudge. When he put the *Western Slope* to sea again he gave command to Bill Moore, with Henry as mate and J. W. as purser. He also gave command of the *Princess Louise* to W. D. Moore, so the family was well looked after. J. W. Moore remained a purser with the Canadian Pacific Navigation Company, and its successor, the B.C. Coast Steamship Service of the C.P.R., for the rest of his life. Captain William Meyer also became a valued skipper with the C.P.N. Co.

But Captain Moore, senior, was far from ready to become a mere salaried employee. He had scarcely lost control of the *Western Slope* when the *Victoria Colonist* announced that the keel of a new steamboat had been laid at Victoria for Captain William Meyer, who was acting as a front for his father-in-law. The new ship was to have a length of 130 feet and a speed of 14 knots.

Due to lack of finances there were many delays in construction, and when she was finally launched in 1884 as the screw steamer *Teaser,* she was only 83 feet long. Her name was appropriate, for Captain Bill Moore intended to run her as an opposition steamboat to Captain Irving between Victoria and New Westminster. She made a few trips, but Captain Moore's creditors were on his heels. He quarrelled violently with his partners in the enterprise, and they threatened to foreclose.

Captain Moore decided to steal his ship from the clutches of his tormentors. He conceived the idea of sailing her to Petropavlovsk, far away on the Kamchatka Peninsula, selling her to the Russians and pocketing the proceeds. The legality of the matter didn't seem to bother him. He had built the *Teaser* and he felt she belonged to him. Late in 1885, with his son Billie in command, she slipped secretly out of Victoria and up the Inside Passage to Alaska, bound for Siberia.

Captain Moore's creditors in Victoria were left with only an empty space at the dock. Unfortunately for Moore, he was forced to stop at Tongass, Alaska, for fuel. Since Billie was short of funds he had to stay there until he could get credit. This delay gave time for word of the *Teaser* to get back to Victoria.

The creditors sent a deputy sheriff and she was arrested and brought back ignominiously to Victoria. On January 11, 1886, she was sold at a mortgage sale for only $5,500, leaving nothing for the Moore family out of the enterprise. The *Teaser* was subsequently lengthened and renamed *Rainbow*, and passed to the ownership of the Canadian Pacific Navigation Co.

While the *Teaser* was trying to dodge creditors in Alaska, Captain Moore, his son, Ben, and Captain Meyer were in Seattle building still another steamer. This was the 80-foot sternwheeler *Alaskan*, which they built under contract with Calbreath, Grant and Cook, the Cassiar merchants. Early in May 1886 they sailed this fragile little craft up the coast to Fort Wrangell, which was no longer the rip-snorting wild-west town of Cassiar gold rush days.

Since other steamboats had left the Stikine because of declining trade, Captain Moore had the river to himself again, just as he had in the roaring days of 1862 with the *Flying Dutchman.* Captain Moore's fortune was again at very low ebb. After all his years of effort, the *Alaskan* was scarcely better than his first steamer, and he didn't even own her. That season he and Ben ran the *Alaskan* between Wrangell and Telegraph Creek, about 150 miles, with freight for Calbreath, Grant and Cook at $80 a ton. But by August the short season was over and the Moores returned to Victoria.

When things went badly for the Moore family they always set out to look for that elusive gold at the foot of the rainbow. There were no new gold strikes in sight in British Columbia, so in 1886 Captain Moore made his way across the rugged Chilkoot Pass into the great valley of the Yukon River — at that time scarcely explored. Tragically, Henry Moore also heard the call of the Yukon in 1886 and set out with three other young men from Seattle in a schooner called the *Sea Bird.* They never reached the promised land, for all were murdered on Vancouver Island. They anchored their schooner in Blinkinsop Bay to wait for the turn of the tide before entering Johnstone Strait. Apparently while they slept they were killed by Indians who sank their schooner with the bodies. It was a great blow for Captain Bill Moore who dearly loved his family. Henry was 25 and left a wife and 4 children.

In 1887 the fortunes of Captain Bill Moore were at their lowest ebb. He and his sons had accumulated a fortune of approximately $80,000 in the Cassiar mines plus another $10,000 in building the

The White Pass which Captain Moore discovered became the major entry point to Yukon, first by trail, then a railway and today a highway. During the Klondike rush most of the stampeders treated their horses with extreme brutality. Of some 3,000 used in 1897, virtually every one died of starvation, falling off cliffs, or being abandoned among the rocks and snow when they could no longer carry their burdens.

trail from Glenora to Dease Lake. It had all been invested in steamboats and slipped away with the decline of the Stikine trade and the ruinous competition on the Fraser River. All the Captain had left was his unquenchable faith in himself and his belief that there were other fortunes to be won on the distant horizon — even for 65-year-old men.

Letters from his son, Billie, told him of the gold that would some day be won from the Yukon country and he read them avidly. So did his youngest son, Ben, who boarded the mail steamer *Idaho* at Victoria on March 11, 1887, determined to make his fortune in the new north. He was bound for Fortymile Creek, 50 miles below the future site of Dawson on the Yukon River, where there were rumors of a new gold strike.

The traditional Moore magnet was at work again. Captain Moore contracted to go into the Yukon country that summer with a Canadian government survey party headed by William Ogilvie. He was to provide the necessary know-how of packing over wilderness trails and build and navigate a barge with supplies down the Yukon River, a rather formidable assignment for a man of 65.

Entry into the Upper Yukon Valley was via the Chilkoot Trail, a precipitous route that taxed men's strength and courage to the utmost. The old man had heard that there was another route into the Upper Yukon, 600 feet less in altitude, that could be reached from Skagway Bay. He was determined to test the feasibility of the new route, so while the Ogilvie party took the old trail, Captain Moore started up the Skagway River.

Accompanied by an Indian named Skookum Jim — who was later to become world famous as a co-discoverer of the Klondike goldfield — he struggled up over a pass 45 miles long. There was no trail of any kind and travelling entailed perilous switchbacks over precipitous hillsides and canyons. It took them days to join the Ogilvie party at Lake Bennett, one of the headwaters of the mighty Yukon on the B.C.-Yukon border. Moore was enthusiastic about the new route he had discovered. Ogilvie called it the White Pass, after Thomas White, Canadian Minister of the Interior.

As Olgilvie recalled later, the old man's imagination was inspired. "Every night during the two months he remained with us, he would picture the tons of yellow dust yet to be found in the Yukon Valley. He decided then and there that Skagway would be the entry point to the golden fields ... and the White Pass would reverberate with the rumble of railway trains carrying supplies."

Captain Moore's predictions proved amazingly accurate. In 1896 gold was discovered on a river the world came to know as the Klondike, triggering the greatest stampede in history. In the winter of 1897-98 some 30,000 men battled their way over White and Chilkoot Passes, then in spring drifted down the Yukon River in an armada of over 7,000 boats carrying some 30 million pounds of supplies.

Within 10 years the creeks yielded $100 million in gold and eventually produced over $200 million. In 1898 construction started on a railway from Skagway to a new community called Whitehorse in the Yukon, climbing through the Coast Mountains via the perilous White Pass that Captain Moore discovered.

Captain Moore remained with the Ogilvie survey most of the summer, assisting to build a scow and boating down the Yukon River through Miles and Whitehorse Canyons. Not far above the mouth of the Pelly River the party met three men poling up the Yukon. One was Ben Moore, who during the summer had piloted the small sternwheel steamer *New Racket* down the Yukon River from Fortymile to St. Michael on the Bering Sea, a voyage of over 2,000 miles.

Ben has described this reunion with his father:

"I noticed a large scow moored to the left bank of the river with several Peterborough canoes tied to the scow. The weather was very hot, and the mosquitoes thick and furious, which made poling against the swift stream all the more difficult. Through the overhanging willows I soon perceived several men, among whom was William Ogilvie, at that time in charge of a survey into the Yukon for the Canadian government. I next noticed someone along the verge of the river, hurrying toward my boat and fighting mosquitoes with both hands. On nearer approach, I saw it was my father."

It was now August 12, late in the season for that part of the world. Captain Moore decided to leave the Ogilvie party and return to the coast with his son. They forwarded some provisions with Mr. Ogilvie to another Moore son, Billie, who intended to remain at Fortymile for the winter. Ben and his companions had a flat-bottomed boat which they poled and hauled from Fortymile. It was a back-breaking job, but the worst was yet to come — the transit of Whitehorse and Miles Canyons. Ben Moore described the ordeal in his diary. The date was August 26, 1887:

"Started at 4.30 a.m. Towed our boat up through the White Horse after portaging all our luggage. Took the boat through on our right hand side. The water appeared to be fairly high. The boat swamped on us once, but we got her through all right and loaded all our outfit aboard again and poled up through two miles of very swift water, or what many call rapids; then reached the foot of the Miles Canyon. Here we portaged all our outfit again over the hill on our left hand side for a distance of about one mile. We also portaged our boat here, for it was impossible to tow or line a boat through this canyon.

"We lashed two poles about ten feet long across the boat, one a few feet from the bow and the other a few feet from the stern, and by taking out all the oars, paddles, and her inside bottom boards we walked and dragged her right along.

"Arrived at the head of the canyon with all our stuff and boat at 4 p.m. and camped there for the night."

On September 5 they arrived at Lake Lindeman in British Columbia, head of the Yukon waterway, and for Ben the end of 600 tedious miles of rowing and poling from Fortymile Creek. Only the Chilkoot Pass remained to be overcome. He and his father cached their excess baggage 12 feet up a spruce tree, hauled the boat up on shore, and loaded packs on their backs. Ben and his father each carried about 60 pounds and in the teeth of a southwest gale, with heavy rain, started over the dread Chilkoot trail.

They reached the summit at 4.30 p.m. but were unable to proceed further because of the rain-swollen, impassable streams.

"Darkness was about us now," wrote Ben, "and we were cold, hungry, and wet to the skin, and all our blankets were wet except one roll of bedding that my father had wrapped in a canvas covering which was partially dry. We lay down in the rain, in a clump of willows on the wet soggy ground near the creek, and shivered and partially steamed ourselves till morning, without fire or hot drink."

Next morning they forded the creek at 5 a.m. and arrived at Sheep Camp worn out, cold, wet and hungry. It was Ben Moore's 22nd birthday. They dried their clothing and blankets by a camp fire and ate what they had left, some hardtack biscuits, washed down by coffee. Next day they completed their transit of the pass, and arrived at the Dyea trading post, wet through and with empty stomachs. Here they were treated to a hot meal by Mrs. John Healey, wife of the trader, and Ben wrote in his diary: "Never before has a meal tasted so good as this one."

They started out in a canoe for Juneau, and as they passed Skagway Bay, the Captain pointed out the low pass that led through the mountains into the interior. He noted also that the bay had good natural facilities for a wharf. It was bound to be the entry point to the Yukon, he declared, and they must act quickly to take advantage of it.

On their arrival at Juneau, Ben got a temporary job in the Treadwell Mine, while his father followed up his dream for Skagway Bay. He was determined to take up a land pre-emption of 160 acres. Although the stampede of 1898 was still 11 years in the future, Captain Moore correctly foresaw the gold that would be discovered and the main routes that would lead to it.

To hasten the carving of his niche in the wilderness, he procured a canoe, provisions, a tent and some tools. The season was late but Captain Moore felt that no time should be wasted. He could already see in his imagination the deepsea ships that would land at his wharf to unload their thousands of gold seekers.

He and Ben made the canoe journey back to Skagway Bay in conditions that would be considered incredible by most people, but for the Moores was a way of life. They left on October 7, 1887. The journey took a week, during which time both the wind and the rain never stopped.

When they finally reached Lynn Canal the weather changed — the wind now increased to gale force. The narrow inlet became a foaming mass of water and they were forced to find shelter up the mouth of a small river. Here they watched helplessly while two Indians in a large canoe disappeared before their eyes. And still the

Lynn Canal which Captain Moore and his son, Ben, challenged in a canoe has drowned hundreds of people. The worst tragedy was the CPR steamship *Princess Sophia*. In October 1881 she struck Vanderbilt Reef in a snowstorm and gale winds which prevented rescue ships from helping. On the night of October 25 the vessel was blown off the rocks. Of 343 men, women and children on board, none survived.

wind blew and the rain poured down. On October 17 Ben noted in his diary:

"Before daybreak we had to rush out of our tent and away from the standing timber, because many trees were falling, torn up by the roots and some breaking in two, and within an hour the gale had increased to a hurricane, whirling into our faces."

Not until three days later did the weather clear sufficiently for them to hoist a sail on their canoe and slip into the shelter of Skagway Bay. Here they camped on the beach, first white settlers in this primeval wilderness.

Captain Moore made a dramatic gesture on their arrival. When Ben struck his axe into the first tree his father declaimed: "Here we will cast our future lots and try to hew out our fortune."

Ben never forgot the words, and no wonder, for no matter how rough the going, the old man never lost sight of his goal. Later he said to his son:

"I fully expect before many years to see a pack trail through this pass, followed by a wagon road, and I would not be at all surprised to see a railroad through to the lakes." Thirteen years later the railway was operational.

But that was in the future. For now the season was late and the Moores hurriedly prepared to make the dream come true. Within a day of their arrival they sounded the bay to find the most suitable location for a wharf and started cutting logs for cribbing. The terrible weather continued, with snowstorms and frequent gales, yet they worked on the wharf and laid the foundation for a little log house.

After three weeks of toil they decided to return to Juneau in Healey's schooner *Charlie* since there would be no steamboat until the following March. After they paid their Indian helper they had only enough cash for their fares from Juneau to Victoria. The voyage in the schooner was so rough that even Captain Moore was seasick — the first time in 40 years.

During the winter and early spring Captain Moore and his son prepared maps of the various routes into the Yukon for the Provincial Government. They were paid $250, money badly needed to support the household. Captain Moore also wrote voluminous letters to the Dominion Government at Ottawa, setting forth his ideas of the future of the Yukon Territory, its great prospects as a mineral producing area and its valuable fur-bearing animals. He described the thousands of miles of navigable rivers and emphasized the practicability of a pack train or wagon road over the White Pass. His submissions were received with indifference.

CHAPTER FIVE

Captain Moore spent the 1890 season in the south, but he was back in Alaska in 1891, working on his Skagway property and freighting with the *Flying Dutchman* for the canneries and trading posts in the Lynn Canal area. That year he presented a petition to the United States Secretary of the Interior asking for the franchise to construct a toll road over the White Pass from tidewater to Lake Bennett, but it was not granted.

He also worked for the Canadian Government that season, in-

Captain Moore in front of his Skagway house which he built in 1892, six years before the Klondike rush. It is decorated for the Fourth of July .

The community of Fortymile on the Yukon River was established several years before the Klondike gold rush. In 1896 the 74-year-old Moore won a contract to deliver mail through 600 miles of wilderness to the community. He received $600 for the 1,200-mile round trip.

Skagway in 1901, with Moore's wharf at left against the bank. It was a massive undertaking, built by hand across the tidal flats to deep water. Some of the boulders rolled into the structure weighed a ton. At the time Skagway was an unknown wilderness, the ever optimistic Moore building the wharf in his unshakable belief that gold would be discovered in the Yukon.

specting routes into the Interior and procuring a Canadian grant to build a shelter cabin a mile south of Lake Lindeman on the Chilkoot Trail.

He was back in the north during the 1894 season, working for two months on the Skagway Bay pre-emption, where he had two Indians employed. In June he joined his son, Ben, at a sawmill in Berners Bay, where they built a 38-foot centreboard schooner which they called the *Gertrude*. Ben had married a native girl in 1891, and lived permanently in the north thereafter.

He was living at Juneau in January 1895 when seven prospectors arrived from California bound for Hootalinqua (Teslin) River. He took passage with them in the little steamer *Rustler* and persuaded them to land at Skagway instead of Dyea. He helped lighter their five tons of equipment ashore and over the White Pass as far as the second canyon. This was the first party of prospectors to use the White Pass route into the Yukon.

In 1896 Captain Moore secured a Dominion Government contract to deliver Royal Mail from Juneau to Fortymile in the Yukon, the first contract ever awarded for delivery of mail into the Yukon. Fortymile was located about 600 miles downstream from the headwaters of the Yukon River and was the largest settlement in the Yukon, even though it consisted of only some 200 log cabins, the inevitable saloons and an opera house staffed by San Francisco dance-hall girls.

For the formidable task of delivering the mail through 600 wilderness miles, Captain Moore was to receive $600 a round trip. He was now 74, but still as tough and hardbitten as the country he had to challenge. With the assistance of Ben, he fulfilled the mail contract — a remarkable feat of endurance.

He sailed from Juneau on May 26 in the American tug *Sea Lion* for Skagway where he met Ben and arranged for him to handle the second mail delivery of the contract. Accompanied by one white assistant and four natives, the sturdy old captain set out over the Chilkoot Pass, carrying 104 pounds of mail, provisions for the whole trip, and lumber to build a boat on Lake Lindeman.

He then proceeded to sail the entire 2,100-mile length of the Yukon in this flat-bottomed boat, delivering the mail at Fortymile and Fort Cudahy, and continuing down the river to St. Michael, where he took the steamer *Bertha* for San Francisco. He was back in Victoria by August 12 in time to embark on another mail trip.

On this trip he camped at the site of the present community of Dawson City of the Trail of '98 fame. Here he met George Carmack who had a few days before staked a discovery claim on a small creek in a region that would explode on the world as the "Klondike." Its creeks were to lure some 75,000 men northward and in a few years yield $100 million in gold dust and nuggets. Nine years previously Captain Moore had visualized that one day a mighty gold strike would bring fame to the North. His vision was about to come true.

By the time he reached Fortymile, word was beginning to get around about the new discovery. He continued down to Circle City and then returned to Fortymile to pick up the return mails. By now the rush was on, and Moore would certainly have joined in, except for the importance of his mail contract. William Ogilvie was at Fortymile and he gave Captain Moore a brief message to take out, informing the Canadian authorities of the great Klondike find.

One of Moore's prospecting friends staked a claim for him on Hunter Creek, not far from Carmack's claims on Bonanza Creek. Unfortunately, the claim was soon jumped on the grounds that it had not been staked in person. It proved a rich one, but not for Captain Moore. The man who took the claim subsequently paid him $1,000, although he was under no legal obligation.

That winter Captain Moore was full of optimism. For 10 years he had based his hopes for the future on the ultimate development of Skagway Bay as the port of entry to the riches of the Yukon. Now that he knew at first hand about the Klondike he was convinced that at last he had found the elusive pot of gold at the foot of the rainbow. He would wrest wealth not from the Klondike directly, but from the trail that he could see winding over the cliffs and canyons of White Pass.

The third mail journey undertaken by Captain William Moore portrays amazing endurance under adversity. For a man of 74 the hardships borne are hard to believe. Here is his official report to the Canadian Postmaster-General, dated March 1, 1897:

"Sir,—Having just returned to Victoria with the last mail of the summer service entrusted to my care under my arrangement with the department last spring, and having been subjected to many delays with the same, owing to adverse condition of the elements, I beg leave to submit the following report:- I left Victoria with this (the last) mail on the 16th of August, and arrived at Juneau on the 20th, leaving there by steamer for Dyea on the Chilcoot Portage on the 22nd. The steamer was obliged to take shelter for two days on the way, owing to a high gale of wind which prevented us from taking a landing at the latter place. We finally succeeded in making a landing on the 25th under a heavy downpour of rain, during which the native packers refused to work, and the Dyea River had also swollen to such an extent that it was impossible to cross it. I was detained there three days.

"On the 29th I started across the portage to Lake Lindeman, at which point I arrived on the 30th, and next day started down the lakes. The weather was very rainy and blustering during the remainder of my journey, and I finally arrived at my destination at

In 1898 the *Ogilvie* plied the Stikine River under command of Captain Moore's son, Billie, who was an expert riverboatman.

Stampeders bound for the Klondike in 1898 struggle up the Stikine River, explored by Captain Moore and his sons in 1873.

C.E.FRIPP.

STIKINE RIVE

Fort Cudahy on the 11th of September. I waited here four days for the steamer *Arctic*, which was daily expected to arrive on her way to Fort Selkirk, at the mouth of the Pelly, 238 miles above Fort Cudahy.

"Mr. Ogilvie, chief of the Canadian survey party, in whose company I intended to return, was also waiting for her, as he was intending to come out. But as the steamer did not arrive and was long overdue, I became anxious about her, and fearing that some accident might have befallen her, I made up my mind to return by way of the mouth of the river, as I did on my first trip.

"So on the 15th I left Fort Cudahy in a small boat to go down the river. On the 17th I arrived at Circle City, and immediately sought Mr. McQuestion (McQuesten), the Alaska Commercial Company's agent at that place, for information regarding the steamer. He assured me that both the *Arctic* and *Bella* were hourly expected to arrive, and that the *Bella* would return at once to St. Michael's with passengers to connect with the *Bertha*, which would leave the latter place about the end of October. After waiting here eight days and neither steamer arriving, I resolved on continuing my journey down the river, in company with four men in a small boat.

"That night it began to snow and freeze, and it looked as though the winter was closing in upon us. The next morning it was still snowing and blowing so hard that after making a start we were obliged to make a landing and wait for the storm to subside. On the morning of the 27th we made another start, although it was still snowing, and about 10 o'clock we met the steamer *Arctic*. Captain Beeker informed us that the *Bella* was two days behind.

"The next day, the 28th, we met the *Bella* a little below Fort Yukon. Captain Mayo informed us that it would be useless to continue our journey down the river, as the *Bertha* would sail from St. Michael's on October 1st, and that he had orders to put his boat into winter quarters and not try to return to the mouth of the river. I then decided to continue down the river to Nulato and endeavor to cross the country to Nashagak; but as my companions were unwilling to accompany me on account of the perils of such a journey at that time of the year (the winter not being sufficiently advanced) I was perforce obliged to return on the *Bella* to Fort Cudahy.

"I had now to face a winter journey out, for which I commenced to make preparations about the middle of November. After securing dog teams and an outfit I started on the 21st of November up the river; but the latter was not yet safe owing to many open places, and I was, therefore, subjected to some delays. The ice on the river was very rough in some places, but on the whole the travelling was fair. On the 5th of December I arrived back to Fort Cudahy, where I remained six days to replenish my supply of provisions, rest the dogs and make moccasins for their feet ... without which they would not have been able to continue their journey. On the 11th I left Fort Cudahy and three days later arrived at Klondike, where a stay of four days was made owing to the dogs' feet being too sore to travel and also to procure additional supplies of provisions (including 117 lbs. of beef, for which I was obliged to pay 50 cents per lb.

"On the 18th of December I resumed my journey, after securing the services of an Indian to break trail, also two more dogs. My party now consisted of four men and eight dogs. On the 20th Sixty-Mile River was reached, we secured a supply of salmon for dog feed at 40 cents per lb. Pelly River was reached on the 27th, where we stayed four days, as the dogs needed rest, and this was the last place at which we could secure supplies. Here we added nine sacks of flour, some dried fruit and some salmon to our outfit, and on January 1st we started again.

"We had now 400 miles to travel before us, with no opportu-

Dawson City on the Yukon River, the famous Klondike flowing in from the left. In 1896 on what was then a bush-covered flat, Captain Moore met George Carmack just after he, with Tagish Charlie and Skookum Jim, had staked the claims which started the Klondike stampede. The 74-year-old Moore would have joined them and also become rich, but he felt that he had to honor his $600 mail contract.

nity of replenishing our supplies, which consisted of about 1,000 lbs. of provisions for men and dogs. Soon after we started we met Dr. Day, the United States mail carrier, about 15 miles above Pelly Mouth. He had abandoned his sleds as his dogs had given out, and an Indian was hauling his mail sack. On January 10th I overtook the Gillis party, who had left Pelly Mouth a day ahead of me, with the United States mails.

"The next day I overtook another party carrying out an express, also despatches for the Canadian Government. He had left Pelly Mouth 10 days before us, with two Indians and a white man as assistants, and had only two days' provisions to last them a distance of about 220 miles. I was obliged to render him considerable assistance in order to enable him to reach the coast, as his party was in imminent danger of actual starvation.

"On January 26th we reached Lake Bennett, where we met Mr. Hayes carrying in a United States mail. His dogs were in a very

bad condition, and it appeared doubtful if he would succeed in getting through with them. On the 27th we crossed the summit, and on the 28th were camped at salt water. I was obliged to wait here for communication several days, and arrived at my destination at Juneau on the 10th of February. In view of the unexpected delays which rendered a winter trip unavoidable and the greater expenses and vicissitudes of travel incident to the same I would respectfully ask the department to recommend the granting to me of a bonus of, say, $500, to recompense me for the extra expense (having to secure a winter outfit of dogs, etc.) to which I have been put in making this trip. I have the honor to be, sir, your obedient servant, Wm. Moore."

For many years Captain Moore had tried to win financial support for his Skagway venture from the business community of Victoria, but without success. Perhaps too many recalled his sorry financial history. He looked like a poor risk. There was, however, a firm in Victoria called the B.C. Development Co. Ltd., which represented British capitalists who were anxious to invest in British Columbia. Early in 1896, before the Klondike gold discovery, Captain Moore approached E. E. Billinghurst of the B. C. Development Co., who was the agent for an English promoter and capitalist named C. H. Wilkinson.

So persuasive was Captain Moore of the future prospects of Skagway Bay as the gateway for a wagon trail and railway to the Yukon Territory that Mr. Wilkinson arranged to advance the old captain $1,800 for supplies, two horses, a couple of cows, 6,000 feet of rough lumber and other materials. In return the lenders were to have a lien on Moore's preemption at Skagway Bay. The amount wasn't much, but it was the biggest sum of money Captain Moore had seen for many a lean and hungry year. From this humble beginning came the British capital that was to finance the building of Captain Moore's long-cherished railway, the White Pass and Yukon.

The supplies arrived at Skagway in June 1896, and since Billinghurst guaranteed the payment of wages for five men that season, Ben Moore was able to improve the wharf and start a trail over the Pass. Later, 15 men were employed to construct a pack trail along the bank of the Skagway River and canyons with the necessary bridges. The Moores also improved the homestead, built a sawmill and procured a steam pile driver with which they extended the wharf into Skagway Bay.

They were thus prepared for the sudden onslaught of events that occurred in the summer of 1897. On June 5 the Canadian Government published William Ogilvie's report on the wealth of Yukon Territory, chastely called *Information Respecting the Yukon District*. At first it attracted little attention. A month later, when the steamer

Excelsior arrived at San Francisco from St. Michael with passengers laden with nuggets from the Klondike, the gold fever was born.

On July 17 the steamer *Portland* arrived at Seattle from St. Michael, and the Seattle *Post-Intelligencer* carried the famous headline: "Gold! Gold! Gold! Gold! 60 Rich Men on the Steamer *Portland*. Stacks of Yellow Metal!" The paper declared that the vessel had more than a ton of solid gold aboard. Within hours the news was flashed round the world and Captain Moore's dream came true.

Every available ship that could float — and some that couldn't — booked passengers for the new Eldorado, either via St. Michael, in distant Bering Sea, or via Dyea, entry port for the Chilkoot Pass. At first there was no mention of Skagway or White Pass, but the word soon spread that there was an alternative route to the dreaded Chilkoot Trail, and that there was a good wharf at Skagway and a passable trail over the White Pass.

On July 29, 1897, Ben Moore induced Captain James Carroll of the mail steamer *Queen* to use the wharf at Skagway. He landed about 200 passengers and 125 tons of freight. Next to arrive was the *Islander*, skippered by Captain John Irving, old friend and rival of the Moores, followed by a host of other vessels, including the collier *Willamette* with some 800 passengers squeezed into her grimy holds.

Skagway became a town overnight. Captain Moore transferred 60 acres of his original pre-emption to the British Yukon Company, which immediately laid out a townsite. During those early boom days he became the most prominent man in town. Now 75 but still strong and massive, with a flowing beard, he was a striking figure as he moved about his wharf, clad in a heavy yellow overcoat that defied the stormy winds blowing down from the canyons.

There was little law and order at Skagway in those days, and there were many who paid little attention to the rights of the original pre-emptor. Some said he had no legal rights at all and a shanty town grew up that paid no respect to his prior claims of ownership. A crowning indignity occurred when it was discovered that his log cabin was in the middle of one of the newly-surveyed streets. A crowd of toughs tried to eject him from his own home, but the old man held them off with a crowbar while his wife stood sobbing in the doorway.

Land speculators claimed there were irregularities in the registry of his original pre-emption which made all his years of effort in vain. He took them to court and litigation lasted for years. In the end he was awarded 25 per cent of the assessed value of the lots within the townsite, worth about $20,000. The wharf also proved a good investment in the long run, particularly after work began in 1898 on the White Pass and Yukon Railway.

During 1897 Captain Moore's second son, Billie, or W.D., was fishing and trading with the natives of the Lower Yukon River, far away from the fabulous Klondike discoveries. While others got rich, he scarcely scraped out a livelihood. In 1898 he commanded the C.P.R. sternwheeler *Ogilvie* on the Stikine.

Later in the year, with scores of passenger boats running up the Yukon River from St. Michael to Dawson, his services were in great demand as an experienced river navigator. He was employed by the Alaska Commercial Company and kept busy day and night piloting from St. Michael to the mouth of the Yukon River and up the delta to the main channel. He made good money that year and was in an excellent position to take advantage of a new gold strike at Nome in northwestern Alaska on the Berring Sea. He located some claims and sank $9,000 into the venture, but he wasn't about to hit a pay streak.

His old father, still irrepressible, also smelled gold in the sands of Nome and left Skagway on April 27, 1900, for the new diggings. Never in his long life had he resisted a stampede to a new mining camp and he ran true to form.

When he arrived at Nome, however, he learned from Billie that prospects were poor and he soon returned to Skagway. There he built a fine new home for his beloved wife, Hendrika, who had suffered much over the years. He harked back to his old seafaring days, for he built it with a "Texas," or pilothouse, at the top, from which he could look out on the busy shipping activities in Skagway Bay.

Despite his fondness for litigation, he managed to save enough from his Skagway property to have a fairly comfortable old age. He returned to Victoria, and there he died March 29, 1909, aged 87.

J. Bernard Moore, his youngest son, left Skagway in 1906 and moved to Tacoma. Here he lost most of his hard-earned money to shrewd and unscrupulous business sharpies. He died at San Francisco in 1919, aged 54. His elder brother, Captain W. D. Moore, remained in Alaska during the rest of his long life, steamboating on the Yukon River, fishing and trading, and from 1912 to 1923 acting as a watchman at St. Michael. Penniless in his old age, he died in 1945 at the Pioneer Home in Sitka, aged 91.

The four Moore boys were a credit to their father, of whom Captain W. D. Moore wrote in a personal letter in September 1928:

"Father was not an educated man. Had he been so, his life would have read in a different way. He was headstrong and aggressive, full of ambition, never would give up. He used to smoke when he was young. He gave it up. He did not drink to excess. He did not gamble. He was fond of his wife and children."

To which might be added: "He was a giant in his time. A pioneer of pioneers."

A selection of other HERITAGE HOUSE titles:

The PIONEER DAYS IN BRITISH COLUMBIA Series

Every article is true, many written or narrated by those who, 100 or more years ago, lived the experiences they relate. Each volume contains 160 pages in large format magazine size (8½ x 11), four-color covers, some 60,000 words of text and over 200 historical photos, many published for the first time.

A continuing Canadian best seller in three volumes which have sold over 75,000 copies. Each volume, $12.95

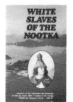

WHITE SLAVES OF THE NOOTKA

On March 22, 1803, while anchored in Nootka Sound on the West Coast of Vancouver Island, the *Boston* was attacked by "friendly" Nootka Indians. Twenty-five of her 27 crew were massacred, their heads "arranged in a line" for survivor John Jewitt to identify. Jewitt and another survivor became 2 of 50 slaves owned by Chief Maquina, never knowing what would come first — rescue or death.

The account of their ordeal, published in 1815, remains remarkably popular. New Western Canadian edition, well illustrated. 128 pages. $9.95

THE DEATH OF ALBERT JOHNSON: Mad Trapper of Rat River

Albert Johnson in 1932 triggered the greatest manhunt in Canada's Arctic history. In blizzards and numbing cold he was involved in four shoot-outs, killing one policeman and gravely wounding two other men before being shot to death.

This revised, enlarged edition includes photos taken by "Wop" May, the legendary bush pilot whose flying skill saved two lives during the manhunt. Another Canadian best seller. $7.95

OUTLAWS AND LAWMEN OF WESTERN CANADA

These true police cases prove that our history was anything but dull. Chapters in 160-page Volume Three, for instance, include Saskatchewan's Midnight Massacre, The Yukon's Christmas Day Assassins, When Guns Blazed at Banff, and Boone Helm — The Murdering Cannibal.

Each of the three volumes in this Canadian best seller series is well illustrated with maps and photos, with four-color photos on the covers. Volume One, $8.95; Volume Two, $8.95; Volume Three, $9.95

B.C. PROVINCIAL POLICE STORIES: Mystery and Murder
from the Files of Western Canada's First Lawmen

The B.C. Police, born in 1858, were the first lawmen in Western Canada. During their 90 years of service they established a reputation as one of the most progressive police forces in North America. All cases in these best selling titles are reconstructed from archives and police files.

Volume One: 16 chapters, many photos, 128 pages. $9.95
Volume Two: 22 chapters, many photos, 144 pages. $9.95
Volume Three: 23 chapters, many photos, 160 pages. $12.95

B.C. BACKROADS

This best selling series contains complete information from Vancouver through the Fraser Canyon to Cache Creek, east to Kamloops country and north to the Cariboo. Also from Vancouver to Bridge River-Lillooet via Whistler. Each book contains mile-by-mile route mileage, history, fishing holes, wildlife, maps and photos.

Volume One — Garibaldi to Bridge River Country-Lillooet. $9.95
Volume Three — Junction Country: Boston Bar to Clinton. $9.95
Thompson-Cariboo: Highways, byways, backroads. $4.95

An Explorer's Guide: MARINE PARKS OF B.C.

To tens of thousands of boaters, B.C.'s Marine Parks are as welcome and convenient as their popular highway equivalents. This guide includes anchorages and onshore facilities, trails, picnic areas campsites, history and other information. In addition, it is profusely illustrated with color and black and white photos, maps and charts.

Informative reading for boat owners from runabouts to cabin cruisers. 200 pages $12.95.

GO FISHING WITH THESE BEST SELLING TITLES

HOW TO CATCH SALMON — BASIC FUNDAMENTALS

The most popular salmon book ever written. Information on trolling rigging tackle, most productive lures, proper depths, salmon habits downriggers, where to find fish, and much more.

Sales over 130,000. 176 pages. $5.95

HOW TO CATCH SALMON — ADVANCED TECHNIQUES

The most comprehensive advanced salmon fishing book available Over 200 pages crammed full of how-to-tips and easy-to-follow diagrams. Covers all popular salmon fishing methods: mooching trolling with bait, spoons and plugs, catching giant chinook, and a creel full of other information.

A continuing best seller. 192 pages. $11.95

HOW TO CATCH CRABS: How popular is this book? This is the 11th printing, with sales over 90,000. $4.95

HOW TO CATCH BOTTOMFISH: Revised and expanded. $5.95

HOW TO CATCH SHELLFISH: Updated 4th printing.
144 pages. $3.95

HOW TO CATCH TROUT by Lee Straight, one of Canada's top outdoorsmen. 144 pages. $5.95

HOW TO COOK YOUR CATCH: Cooking seafood on the boat, in a camper or at the cabin. 8th printing. 192 pages. $4.95

FLY FISH THE TROUT LAKES

with Jack Shaw

Professional outdoor writers describe the author as a man "who can come away regularly with a string when everyone else has been skunked." In this book, he shares over 40 years of studying, raising and photographing all forms of lake insects and the behaviour of fish to them.

Written in an easy-to-follow style. 96 pages. $8.95

SALMON FISHING BRITISH COLUMBIA: Volumes One and Two
Since B.C. has some 7,000 miles of coastline, a problem to its 400,000 salmon anglers is where to fish. These books offer a solution. Volume One includes over 100 popular fishing holes around Vancouver Island. Volume Two covers the Mainland Coast from Vancouver to Jervis Inlet. Both include maps, gear to use, best times, lures and a tackle box full of other information.

Volume One — Vancouver Island. $9.95
Volume Two — Mainland Coast: Vancouver to Jervis Inlet. $11.95

Heritage House books are sold throughout Western Canada. If not available at your bookstore you may order direct from Heritage House, Box 1228, Station A, Surrey, B.C. V3S 2B3. Payment can be by cheque or money order but add 7 per cent for the much hated GST. Books are shipped postpaid.